"A timely reminder of eternal truths. Writing with warmth, care and insight, John Lennox addresses some of the questions and fears many of us are wrestling with right now."

Michael Ramsden, President, Ravi Zacharias International Ministries (RZIM)

"A clear, compassionate and critical read for these times. This book will give those who believe renewed confidence in *why* they believe; and it will help those yet to believe to find the key answers they seek."

Keith and Kristyn Getty, Songwriters

"In the last few months the world has changed. John has written a number of books but none before in the space of a week, as he has this one. Yet despite its brief gestation, this book puts the coronavirus pandemic into a historical, scientific, theological and personal perspective that will help all of us who are in the midst of this crisis to view the situation though a wider-angled lens."

Dr David Cranston, Associate Professor of Surgery, University of Oxford; Governing Body Fellow of Green Templeton College

"No voice in the Western world is clearer and wiser than that of John Lennox. For all who want to pause to think, this is the book to read."

Os Guinness, Author, *Unspeakable* and *Fool's Talk*

"How are we to make sense of a threatening global pandemic that has brought life to a standstill? Where is God? How could he have allowed this? Professor Lennox brings his deep grasp of science and his passionate Christian faith together to reflect on our frightening predicament. This profound but easily accessible book does not claim to have all the answers but certainly addresses the big questions and will help you make sense of the challenges we all face together."

Dr Peter Saunders, CEO, International Christian Medical and Dental Association (ICMDA)

Acknowledgements

I would like to thank those people who have helped
me in various ways with this project: in particular Tim
Thornborough, the indefatigable Publishing Director of The
Good Book Company, its Editorial Director Carl Laferton,
and my research assistant, Dr Simon Wenham.

Where Is God in a Coronavirus World?
© John C. Lennox, 2020

Published by
The Good Book Company

thegoodbook.com | www.thegoodbook.co.uk
thegoodbook.com.au | thegoodbook.co.nz | thegoodbook.co.in

ISBN: 9781784985691 | Printed in the USA

Design by André Parker

Contents

Introduction   5

1. Feeling Vulnerable   7

2. Cathedrals and Worldviews   12

3. Can Atheism Help?   22

4. How Can There Be Coronavirus If There Is a Loving God?   32

5. Evidence of Love   42

6. The Difference God Makes   50

Postscript   62

To a world in pain
JCL

Introduction

We are living through a unique, era-defining period. Many of our old certainties have gone, whatever our view of the world and whatever our beliefs. Whether you are a Christian or not, the coronavirus pandemic is perplexing and unsettling for all of us. How do we begin to think it through and cope with it?

This book consists of my reflections on what we are experiencing right now. I started writing it a week ago, and things have changed quickly since then and no doubt will do again. The views I express here are my own, and should not be attributed to the university or organisations with which I am affiliated. There will, inevitably, be some rough edges and inadequacies. For that I apologise.

I would invite you, the reader, to view the book like this: I am sitting with you in a coffee shop (if only we could!), and you have asked me the question on the book cover. I put down my coffee cup and attempt to give you an honest answer. What follows is what I would try to say to convey some comfort, support and hope.

1. Feeling Vulnerable

I t is quite surreal.

Here I am, in my mid-seventies, sitting at home with my wife, watching a government health minister on television informing us that we may have to remain confined to our home in self-isolation for up to four months in order to try to avoid the coronavirus pandemic that is sweeping the world. (There are many coronaviruses, and this one is called Covid-19, though we shall mostly use the term "coronavirus" in this book.) It is hard to grasp that this pandemic has the potential to be the worst ever, and that all our current estimates of its impact are likely to fall far short of the reality. Its scale and scope sound like something out of a dystopian movie. And yet it is really happening.

Never before have we experienced the lockdown of cities and even countries, the closing of borders, the banning of travel, the shutting of all but essential services, the banning of large sports gatherings, and the silent towns and cities that shout of fear and self-isolation. The rate at which the pandemic is spreading is putting enormous strain on national health systems as the production of necessary resources is stepped up as never before.

Europe has become the centre of a pandemic that originated in China.[1] On the one hand, television news broadcasts feature empty streets, empty shelves in supermarkets, empty sports stadia and empty churches; whereas on the other, hospitals are filling up and extra beds are much in demand. Jobs and businesses are at risk. Fear is stalking the world and it grows by the day as more and more people are affected.

One major effect is the universal feeling of increased vulnerability. Many of us had got used to a fairly stable world, where life was reasonably predictable. Now that all appears to be crumbling away: the things we have always counted on have gone and we are exposed as never before to forces way outside our control. People fear for their health, both physical and psychological; for their families and friends, particularly the elderly and infirm; for their social networks, their food supply, their jobs and economic security, and a host of other things.

In such a shaky and uncertain climate, it is very easy to lose a sense of proportion. After all, we seem to have little difficulty accepting the annual influenza death statistics. Public Health England estimates that, on average, 17,000 people in England have died annually from flu in the past five years; in the US, the Centers for Disease Control and Prevention puts the figure for October 2019 to March 2020 at 23,000-59,000. They also estimate that in 2019 1.35 million people died on roads worldwide. Yet coronavirus scares us more than any of these, because of the vast scale and exponential growth of the virus and its soberly estimated potential to kill untold multitudes of people. I am all too aware that by the time you read this, the numbers who have died of coronavirus will be hugely higher than they are now as I write it.

Francis Collins, the director of the National Institute of Health in the USA, in an interview in *The Atlantic* that is well worth reading in its entirety, explains what most surprised him about this virus:

> *"The degree to which this is so rapidly transmis-*
> *sible. More so than SARS was. SARS was a terribly*
> *scary situation for the world 18 years ago, but it*
> *never reached the level of infections or deaths that*
> *we have for this coronavirus, because it wasn't as*
> *transmissible. SARS was transmissible only from*
> *people who were really very sick. This one seems*
> *to be transmissible from people who have minor*
> *illness or no illness at all..."* [2]

How should we react to all of this? Is it even possible to get it into any kind of proportion? How can we avoid giving way to panic and hysteria?

WE HAVE BEEN HERE BEFORE

There have been similar pandemics in the past. The most ancient recorded instance is probably the so-called

Antonine Plague or Plague of Galen in AD 165-180. The disease involved is uncertain, but is thought to have been measles or smallpox; it killed around five million people. Then there was the Plague of Justinian (AD 541–542). This was a bubonic disease which was spread from animals (rats) via fleas to humans. It is reckoned that over 25 million died.

There was a further bubonic plague, known as the Black Death, in the 14th century (1346-1353), which killed an estimated 70 to 100 million people living in Eurasia—reducing the world population by around 20 percent.

Much later in history, there were several cholera pandemics in the 19th and early 20th centuries in which over a million died. A flu pandemic took the lives of 20 to 50 million in 1918-1920. In my own lifetime, two million died of Asian flu in 1956-1958 and a further million of Hong Kong flu in 1968-1969. The HIV/AIDS pandemic, which was at its peak in 2005-2012, has had a death toll of around 32 million.[3]

These are all classified as pandemics. In addition, there have been many epidemics, like Ebola and SARS, which have been geographically confined and therefore do not qualify as pandemics. As recently as 120 years ago, people in the West lived with epidemics—typhus, tuberculosis, cholera and so on—as a part of normal life.

The coronavirus, like the bubonic plague, is thought to have started with animals and spread to humans.

Yet this is now the 21st century: there has been a vast improvement in understanding of disease and in medicine in recent times, and this has probably had the effect of making many people complacently imagine that pandemics have surely now been relegated to history. Only now are we beginning to realise that they have not. How do we respond to this new circumstance?

IS GOD THERE?

In the past, in times of national disaster in the West, people have flocked into churches and national leaders have made calls for prayer. Such occurrences are rare today, although at least a few national leaders have asked for prayer—as well, of course, as many church leaders around the world. Chief Justice Mogoeng of South Africa has made a memorable appeal: "My call is to all those who can pray, to see it as an absolute necessity starting from today to do so."[4]

But nowadays, fewer and fewer people have any God-dimension whatsoever in their lives. Since all over the world churches are being closed in order to limit the spread of the virus, many are asking where God is—that is, if he is there at all. Is he in inaccessible self-quarantine? Where or from whom can we get real solace or hope?

2. Cathedrals and Worldviews

In times of crisis, hope is what we look for. In a *New York Times* article on 10th March 2020, Italian journalist Mattia Ferraresi wrote the following:

> *"Holy water is not a hand sanitizer and prayer is not a vaccine ... But for believers, religion is a fundamental source of spiritual healing and hope. It's a remedy against despair, providing psychological and emotional support that is an integral part of well-being. (It's also an antidote to loneliness, which several medical experts point to as one of the most worrisome public health issues of our time.)*

> *"At a deeper level, religion, for worshipers, is the ultimate source of meaning. The most profound claim of every religion is to make sense of the whole of existence, including, and perhaps especially, circumstances marked by suffering and tribulation. Take such claims seriously enough, and even physical health, when it is devoid of greater purpose, starts to look like a hollow value."* [5]

When life seems predictable and under control, it is easy to put off asking the big questions, or to be satisfied with simplistic answers. But life is not that way right now—not for any of us. It is not surprising that, whatever your faith or belief system, the big questions of life are breaking through to the surface, demanding attention.

Coronavirus confronts us all with the problem of pain and suffering. This, for most of us, is one of life's hardest problems. Experience rightly makes us suspicious of simplistic answers and facile attempts to come to terms with it.

What I want to try to do here, then, is to avoid those kinds of "answers", and to think with you, as honestly as I can, through some of the ideas that have helped me to wrestle with these difficult questions as coronavirus has begun to change everything.

RUINED CATHEDRALS

You may well ask: why do we need another book on the question of suffering when so many are now available? The answer is that most of these books concentrate on the problem of moral evil. This book instead concentrates on what is called the problem of natural evil. That is, my focus is on fractured nature—principally the coronavirus, but also all kinds of diseases and natural catastrophes like earthquakes and tsunamis.

Pain and suffering come from two distinct sources.

First, there is suffering as a result of natural disasters and diseases, for which humans are not (directly) responsible: earthquakes, tsunamis, cancers and the coronavirus. This leads to the problem of pain or, as it is often called, the problem of natural evil. This terminology is somewhat unfortunate, since the word "evil" has moral connotations and neither earthquakes nor viruses are moral agents.

Second, there is suffering for which men and women are directly responsible: acts of hate, terror, violence, abuse and murder. That leads to the problem of moral evil.

Christchurch Cathedral in New Zealand, Coventry Cathedral in England, and the Frauenkirche in Dresden, Germany are powerful and poignant symbols of these two problems. These three ruined church buildings bear traces of two things. On the one hand, they show evidence of the beauty and elegance they once possessed. On the other hand, they are also marred by the deep scars of catastrophe—an earthquake in Christchurch and bombings in Coventry and Dresden. Each ruined cathedral, therefore, presents a mixed picture of beauty and destruction.

Together they remind us that it is unlikely that there are any easy answers to the deep existential questions that arise from catastrophe. For many at such times, the picture is more than ragged—it is extremely raw. Those of us who stand outside the immediate pain of others run the risk of failing to be sufficiently sensitive to that rawness.

However, there is a difference between Christchurch and Coventry. The cathedral in Christchurch collapsed as a result of the shifting of tectonic plates. The cathedrals in Coventry and Dresden collapsed as a result of war. Some people compared the Christchurch earthquake to 9/11, because it sent a similar shockwave around the nation; but there is a major difference. The destruction of the Twin Towers was not a natural disaster; it was a moral disaster. It was a product of human evil. Earthquakes, meanwhile, are natural, not moral, catastrophes.

Of course, moral and natural evil are sometimes connected. The situation is complicated because one can lead to the other; greedy commercial deforestation may lead to the proliferation of desert, which in turn may lead to malnutrition and disease. But the coronavirus outbreak seems to be a case of natural evil (although moral evil lurks nearby in selfish panic-buying and hoarding of food). Inevitably, conspiracy theorists will seek to put the blame on some human agent. Humans are involved in virus transmission, but not deliberately or selfishly—and the main presumption is that the virus jumped from animals to humans.

That said, there is evidence that the authorities in China initially suppressed reports of a potentially devastating new virus. In the *Guardian* newspaper on 11th March, 2020, Lily Kuo reported from Hong Kong:

> *"Official statements by the Chinese government*
> *to the World Health Organisation reported that*
> *the first confirmed case had been diagnosed*
> *on 8 December. Doctors who tried to raise the*
> *alarm with colleagues about a new disease in late*
> *December were reprimanded. Authorities did not*
> *publicly concede there was human-to-human trans-*
> *mission until 21 January."* [6]

Sadly, Dr Li Wenliang, the Wuhan ophthalmologist who was hailed as a hero in China for raising the alarm about the coronavirus in December 2019, himself died less than two months later as a result of catching the infection.

No doubt there will be recriminations and counter-recriminations for each country's reaction to the coronavirus for a long time to come. But none of that will help deal with the crisis, nor help us know how best to react personally.

How we respond will inevitably depend to an extent on our perspective. The way coronavirus appears to an elderly infected woman, hovering between life and death in intensive care, is very different from how it looks to the doctor who is treating her, or to the family member who is unable to visit her, or to the pastor who is trying to help her. Another concern for many of us is whether we have it, or have had it; and whether we could pass it, or have passed it, on to anyone else.

We each need to make sense of coronavirus in three different ways: intellectually, emotionally and spiritually. All are important—and together they present a formidable challenge to anyone.

We all wish to have intellectual clarity, and many people will spend hours watching news programmes and trawling the internet in the hope of gleaning some new piece of information that may help them understand what is happening. However, intellectual analysis does not easily penetrate a veil of tears. How does one bring sense—or if not sense, then perhaps hope—in situations that are devastating and indeed irreversible? The deep questions flow in an unending stream, and perhaps they are a torrent for you as you read this. Why has this happened to me, or to them? Why did they get infected and die, and I was spared? Where can I find alleviation of my physical and mental pain? Is there hope?

WHAT PAIN DOES

Human experience and elementary medicine teach us that pain has an important role to play in our lives. First, pain warns us of danger. If, for example, you put your hand too near the fire, your nervous system alerts your brain and you feel pain, which makes you withdraw your hand and so protects it from injury. We cannot say, then, that pain is all bad.

Second, a certain amount of pain is involved in physical development. For instance—if athletics, mountaineering or the physically demanding games of American football, British rugby and boxing are anything to go by—sports enthusiasts will put up with a great deal of pain in order to excel.

Third, at a deeper level still, suffering and pain can contribute to character formation. There are many examples of resilience and fortitude in the face of suffering—moulding characters of great quality. There is truth in what the Russian author Fyodor Dostoevsky had his character Raskolnikov say: that he could not imagine a great person who had not suffered. "Pain and suffering are always inevitable for a large intelligence and a deep heart."[7]

Parents are often aware of this. On occasion, they will allow a child to go through a painful experience that, they know from their own journey, will profit their child in the end.

I do not claim to know much about this, but let me speak personally for a moment. Some years ago, pain in my chest told me that something was badly wrong. I was rushed into hospital, where the situation was deemed so serious that I had to say goodbye to my wife. Skilful medical intervention saved me in the nick of time from a massive heart attack that would, in all probability, have been fatal. In a sense, I had had an earthquake in my heart.

That kind of experience will leave no one unchanged. For me, it taught me a great deal. It taught me that I was mortal and that I was vulnerable; and I now feel that my life was given back to me as a precious gift to be treasured. It brought more urgency into my sense of purpose and calling.

DISASTERS AND WORLDVIEWS

At almost the same time as my near-fatal heart attack, my sister lost her (just) married 22-year-old daughter to a malignant brain tumour. If I am going to thank God for my recovery—as I do—what shall I say about God to my sister? And what shall I say about God when it comes to a pandemic like coronavirus, where we can see no positive dimension whatsoever—only unrelieved disaster?

C.S. Lewis once wrote a letter that will resonate with most of us:

"It is so difficult to believe that the travail [troubles] of all creation which God himself descended to share may be necessary in the process of turning finite creatures (with free wills) into... well, into gods." [8]

And we could now add the coronavirus to the list.

That letter was written by a one-time atheist who became a Christian in middle age and who explored the problems of pain, suffering and evil in two books: *The Problem of Pain* and *A Grief Observed*. They both illustrate the fact that our attitude to these deep issues is influenced by our worldview—the framework, built up over the years, which contains the thinking and experience that each of us brings to bear on the big questions about life, death and the meaning of existence. We all have such a framework, however much or little we have thought about it.

James Sire, in a very helpful book entitled *The Universe Next Door*, points out that there are essentially only three major families of worldviews.[9] First, there is the theistic worldview, held by the three Abrahamic religions—Judaism, Christianity and Islam. This teaches that there is a God who created and upholds the world and who created human beings in his image. (Notice that I said "families" of worldviews: there are crucial variants within each category, as any Jew, Christian or Muslim who takes their holy book seriously will tell you.)

Second, there is the polar opposite of the theistic approach—the atheistic worldview, which holds that this universe (or multiverse) is all that there is; there is no supernatural dimension. Third, there is the pantheistic worldview, which merges the concepts of God and the world into one impersonal entity.

I am also well aware that there are people who take a sceptical or agnostic perspective. But no one is sceptical or agnostic about everything, and so deep down most people fit somewhere into one of the three worldviews just mentioned.

I fit into this picture too. I have a worldview. I am a Christian, and I shall therefore try to make clear why I think that Christianity has something to say about the issue of natural disasters like coronavirus—something that is not to be found elsewhere. Perhaps you will agree with me, and perhaps not. But I hope you will end this book understanding why Christians are able to speak confidently about hope and to feel a sense of peace, even in a world of uncertainty in which death has suddenly loomed closer.

3. Can Atheism Help?

Your worldview will make a difference to how you react to disasters like the coronavirus pandemic, and to earthquakes or tsunamis. For example, many theists responded to the New Zealand quake by affirming their faith in God in the words of Psalm 46:

> *"God is our refuge and strength,*
>   *an ever-present help in trouble.*
> *Therefore we will not fear, though the earth give way*
>   *and the mountains fall into the heart of the sea,*
> *though its waters roar and foam*
>   *and the mountains quake with their surging."*
>
> (verses 1-3)

Other theists say that pandemics, earthquakes and tsunamis are a direct judgment of God—as indeed people of various religions suggested in the case of the earthquakes and tsunamis in Japan (in 2011) and New Zealand (in 2016). This is a very crude response that causes a lot of unnecessary hurt.

Related to that view, one of the fundamental beliefs to be found in pantheism is that those who suffer do so because of their sin in a previous life, and that suffering in their present life serves to help them to work off their karma.[10] Therefore, since the chain of cause and effect is unbreakable, there is no point in making an effort to relieve their pain; that would only serve to slow down the process of their purification. It is hard to see how this worldview offers any hope at all to people suffering from coronavirus or any other disease. To complicate matters even further, some Eastern philosophies see suffering as a mere illusion.

According to the Bible, it is not true that if someone suffers some severe illness or accident, we should conclude that he or she has secretly been guilty of serious sins. Popular thought has often imagined that this must be the Bible's standpoint. But the whole book of Job in the Old Testament is a protest against that idea. God himself tells Job's friends, who think that Job is responsible for his own suffering, that they are wrong.[11]

Furthermore, Job's pain and suffering are caused by a mixture of natural and moral evil. The source of the attacks on Job's family are two murderous raids by Sabeans and Chaldeans (moral evil) and two natural disasters of fire and wind (natural evil). (I stress again that the word "evil" here does not mean that the source of suffering is immoral—a fire has no morality in itself—but indicates that the damage it does can be described as bad or evil for those affected.)[12]

Jesus likewise explicitly denied that suffering was necessarily connected with personal wrongdoing.[13] Again, as in Job, the context is directly relevant to the topics of both natural and moral evil. The historian Luke, who wrote a historical biography of Jesus (we usually call this "Luke's Gospel" or simply "Luke"), relates the incident:

> *"There were some present at that time who told Jesus about the Galileans whose blood Pilate had mixed with their sacrifices. Jesus answered, 'Do you think that these Galileans were worse sinners than all the other Galileans because they suffered this way? I tell you, no! But unless you repent, you too will all perish. Or those eighteen who died when the tower in Siloam fell on them—do you think they were more guilty than all the others living in Jerusalem? I tell you, no! But unless you repent, you too will all perish.'" (Luke 13 v 1-5)*

Having had his attention called to people who had suffered a state-inflicted atrocity (moral evil), Jesus in turn recalled people who had died in a natural disaster (natural evil); and then, with regard to *both* cases, he rebuked the popular opinion that the victims of these extraordinary things must have been exceptionally outrageous sinners whom God was specifically punishing. The implication is that we live in a world where such things can and do happen, but their occurrence is not always directly caused by God, even though he is sovereign over all things.

We must not miss, though, Jesus' final comment on that occasion, which shows us that there is more to this issue—someone being spared what befalls others does not mean that they are innocent: "Unless you repent, you too will all perish." (We shall explore the matter of repentance later.)

All this said, it is clearly a part of Christian teaching that although not all disaster and disease is a judgment of God (as in the case of Job), nevertheless some is. The early Christian leader Paul told the Corinthian church that some of their number were ill as a consequence of God's judgment: God wanted to get them to repent of an immoral lifestyle.[14] But Paul was writing with the special insight of one who was inspired by God's Spirit. We do not have the same authority to decide who is being punished in this way. Beware of anyone who interprets pain caused by natural evil as a divine punishment. But equally, beware also of anyone who says that God has nothing to say through this pandemic, particularly to Western societies that have largely turned their back on him as culturally irrelevant.

WHY ATHEISM CAN'T HELP YOU

It is worth observing that some atheists believe in some sort of "judgment" or "fate"—it is what lies behind the phrase "they had it coming to them".

And mentioning atheists bring me to the fact that many people think that the only solution to the problem of catastrophe and natural evil is to abandon God and embrace atheism. Surely, they say, coronavirus, cancers, tsunamis and earthquakes show us that there is no God. We must face the fact that this is just the way the universe is: hard and unfeeling, caring nothing for whether we live or die.

The Scottish Enlightenment philosopher David Hume pointed out the problems that Christians like me must wrestle with. Referring to a Greek philosopher from the 3rd century BC, he made this widely quoted statement:

> "Epicurus's old questions are yet unanswered. Is [God] willing to prevent evil, but not able? Then is he impotent. Is he able but not willing? Then is he malevolent. Is he both able and willing? Whence then is evil?" [15]

But where does this atheist path end up? It is but a short step from this to the dogmatic atheistic reaction of Richard Dawkins to the reality of suffering:

> "The total amount of suffering per year in the natural world is beyond all decent contemplation. During the minute that it takes me to compose this sentence, thousands of animals are being eaten alive, many others are running for their lives, whimpering with fear, others are slowly being devoured from within by rasping parasites, thousands of all kinds are dying of starvation, thirst, and disease. It must be so. If there ever is a time of plenty, this very fact will automatically lead to an

increase in the population until the natural state
of starvation and misery is restored. In a universe
of electrons and selfish genes, blind physical forces
and genetic replication, some people are going to get
hurt, other people are going to get lucky, and you
won't find any rhyme or reason in it, nor any justice.
The universe that we observe has precisely the
properties we should expect if there is, at bottom,
no design, no purpose, no evil, no good, nothing but
blind, pitiless indifference. DNA neither knows nor
cares. DNA just is. And we dance to its music." [16]

How does a Christian react to this? The first thing to say is that Dawkins' deterministic version of atheism seems here to abolish the categories of good and evil and replace them with blind, pitiless indifference in a fatalistic universe. However, rejecting good and evil implies that any talk of the coronavirus being bad or evil makes no sense (though it is hard to imagine that Dawkins could actually believe that).

Yet Dawkins is making a serious point, in the light of which we must ask if the atheistic belief system is even a reasonable reaction to the coronavirus. If there is no God, where do the concepts of good and bad that all of us possess come from in the first place? We are left unable to say that the coronavirus and its effects are in any sense "bad", because its consequences, including the fatalities it inflicts, are simply atoms rearranging themselves.

Fyodor Dostoevsky wrote, "If God does not exist,

everything is permissible".[17] To avoid any misunderstanding, it needs to be said that Dostoevsky did not mean that atheists could not behave morally. That is obviously not the case. In fact atheists can, and often have, put religious people to shame by their moral behaviour. The Christian perspective on this is that all men and women, whether or not they believe in God, are moral beings made in the image of a Creator God. All humans, therefore, can behave morally. Dostoevsky was not accusing atheists of a lack of moral conviction. He was rather suggesting something deeper—that there is no rational warrant for the concepts of good and evil if there is no God. Richard Dawkins' statement supports that completely.

Although natural and not moral evil is our principal topic here, it is worth noting in passing that in Dawkins' view, terrorists and the architects of genocide in the killing fields of Cambodia and Rwanda were simply carrying out their own inbuilt genetic programmes: likewise Stalin, Hitler and Mao in their horrific crimes against humanity. If you felt like murdering children for fun, would that not (on this view) simply be dancing to your DNA? If that is so, then none of us can help being what some people misguidedly call evil. We, and they, might as well just resign ourselves to it without complaint. Morality is meaningless.

This view is, I think, simply not livable. Richard Dawkins is himself evidence of this. His argument undermines the reality of such a thing as good and evil; but then why does he then seem to consider 9/11 and other atrocities as evil?[18]

The next thing to note is that justifiable outrage against natural or moral evil presupposes a standard of "good" that is objectively real and independent of us, so that we expect others to agree with us in condemning certain things. These standards are "transcendent"—that is, they exist above the level of individual opinions. For example, all of us, irrespective of our worldview, surely have no hesitation in saying that the coronavirus is bad.

If, however, there is no God, and therefore there are no transcendent values, then how can there be any objective standard of good? If there is no good or evil in any case, the concept of morality disappears, and moral outrage is absurd. The so-called "problem" of evil—moral or natural—dissolves into the pitiless indifference of uncaring matter.

Richard Taylor, a philosopher, agrees:

> *"The modern age, more or less repudiating the idea of a divine lawgiver, has nevertheless tried to retain the ideas of moral right and wrong, not noticing that, in casting God aside, they have also abolished the conditions of meaningfulness for moral right and wrong as well ... Educated people do not need to be told, however, that questions such as these have never been answered outside of religion."* [19]

The nineteenth-century philosopher Friedrich Nietzsche saw more clearly than anyone else the consequences of abandoning the biblical morality that is at the heart of Western civilization. He predicted that the death of God would lead to a Darwinian imperative of expressing the "will to power"—that is, that the strong must and would eliminate the weak. He wrote:

> "The biblical prohibition: 'Thou shalt not kill'
> is a piece of naiveté … Life itself recognizes no
> solidarity, no 'equal rights' between the healthy
> and the degenerate parts of an organism: one must
> excise the latter—or the whole will perish." [20]

Nietzsche despised Christian morality as that of slaves and pointed out that the death of God would mean the death of compassion, kindness and forgiveness:

> "When one gives up Christian belief one thereby
> deprives oneself of the right to Christian morality
> … Christian morality is a command: its origin is
> transcendental … it possesses truth only if God is
> truth—it stands or falls with the belief in God." [21]

In another book Nietzsche then asked the question, "Why morality at all, when life, nature, and history are 'non-moral'?"[22] That is the question with which every atheist must wrestle.

THE PROBLEM FOR CHRISTIANITY

The fact is that morality exists. We know ourselves to be moral beings by direct experience. Prominent Oxford ethicist J.L. Mackie wrote:

> "[Ethics] constitute so odd a cluster of qualities and relations that they are most unlikely to have arisen in the ordinary course of events, without an all-powerful god to create them. If, then, there are such intrinsically prescriptive objective values, they make the existence of a god more probable than it would have been without them. Thus we have, after all, a defensible argument from morality to the existence of a god." [23]

Mackie himself was an atheist who denied the existence of such absolute moral standards. Yet surely, we all can see that some things, like torturing infants, are just wrong—absolutely wrong. Being able to say so is what we give up if we embrace atheism and are willing to follow its logic.

Removing God from the equation does not remove the pain and suffering. It leaves them untouched. But removing God does remove something else—namely, any kind of ultimate hope. This is an issue to which we shall later return.

But we have not yet wrestled with the question that David Hume effectively posed: can the coronavirus be reconciled with the existence of a loving God?

4. How Can There Be Coronavirus If There Is a Loving God?

In order to tackle this question (which will take the next two chapters) we are going first to think about three things: first, the nature of viruses in general; second, the nature of humanity; and third, what the Bible says about why things are the way they are.

THE NATURE OF VIRUSES

To help us think about viruses, here are excerpts of an instructive article from the World Economic Forum written by Peter Pollard, an associate professor at the Australian Rivers Institute, Griffith University. Pollard says:

> "The word 'virus' strikes terror into the hearts of most people. It conjures up images of influenza, HIV, Yellow Fever, or Ebola. Of course we worry about these viruses—they bring us disease and sometimes an excruciatingly painful death.

> "But the 21 viral types that wreak havoc with the human body represent an insignificant fraction of

the 100 million viral types on earth. Most viruses are actually vital to our very existence ...

"The sheer number of these 'good' viruses is astonishing. Their concentration in a productive lake or river is often 100 million per millilitre— that's more than four times the population of Australia squeezed into a ¼ of a teaspoon of water ... Viruses are not living organisms. They are simply bits of genetic material (DNA or RNA) covered in protein, that behave like parasites. They attach to their target cell (the host), inject their genetic material, and replicate themselves using the host cells' metabolic pathways ... Then the new viruses break out of the cell—the cell explodes (lyses), releasing hundreds of viruses...

"It's the combination of high bacterial growth and viral infection that keeps ecosystems functioning ... Thus viruses are a critical part of inorganic nutrient recycling. So while they are tiny and seem insignificant, viruses actually play an essential global role in the recycling of nutrients through food webs. We are only just now beginning to appreciate the extent of their positive impact on our survival.

"One thing is for sure, viruses are our smallest unsung heroes." [24]

Likewise, in an article entitled "Viruses deserve a better reputation", Pennsylvania State University viral ecologist Marilyn Roossinck says that viruses are essential to life, and that at most 1% (a high estimate) of them are pathogenic—that is, harmful to their hosts.

So viruses are in the main beneficial, but a small proportion of them, like Covid-19, are harmful to humans. Covid-19 is one of a large family of coronaviruses that are responsible for the common cold, influenza, pneumonia and other respiratory diseases.

This turns out to be very similar to the situation with earthquakes. In their book *Rare Earth*, geologist Peter Ward and astronomer Donald Brownlee, both of the University of Washington, have a chapter entitled "The Surprising Importance of Plate Tectonics".[25] Its argument is that, if the earth's tectonic plates ceased to move, mass extinction of life on earth would eventually ensue. There are several reasons for this. Plate tectonics is essential for the formation of continents and maintenance of the balance between earth (mountains) and sea. It also acts as a global thermostat by recycling chemicals crucial to maintaining a uniformly balanced level of carbon dioxide.

Furthermore, Ward and Brownlee argue that plate tectonics maintains the earth's magnetic field, which protects it from cosmic rays that would be fatal for life. Their conclusion is this: "It may be that plate tectonics is the central requirement for life on a planet and that it is necessary for keeping a world supplied with water."

Both viruses and earthquakes, then, would appear to be essential for life. If there is a Creator God, he is by definition ultimately responsible for their existence.

Yet why do they have to exist at all? Surely it is not enough to say—as some might—that the coronavirus pandemic is just biology doing what biology does? Surely there must be more to it than that?

Granted that the science shows us that most viruses are beneficial and some are essential to life, why do there have to be pathogens that wreak havoc? The key question for theists is this: could God not have made a world without viral pathogens?

This brings us to a whole class of similar questions. Couldn't God have made electricity that was not dangerous or fire that did not burn? Couldn't God have made an organic world without predation? Couldn't God have made life that never went wrong and viruses that were always beneficial? Couldn't God have made creatures that never did wrong? (After all, though coronavirus is serious, it is not going to kill as many people this year as other people will.)

THE NATURE OF HUMANITY

The last of these questions is, perhaps, somewhat more answerable than the others. The answer to it is clearly yes. Indeed, God has made things that never do moral wrong. Animals, for instance, are not moral beings. If a lion mauls a zoo-keeper, the lion is not charged with murder. It is an a-moral creature.

God could have made a world of robots that simply automatically followed their inbuilt programmes. But that world would not have contained us human beings. In fact, people who wish they inhabited a world without the possibility of evil are actually wishing themselves out of existence. The reason is that one of the greatest gifts that God has given us is that of free will. We can say yes or no, and that capacity opens up wonderful things: love, trust and genuine relationships with God and each other. However, that very same wonderful and good capacity makes us capable of evil, even though it does not give us permission to do evil.

This is a very important point, which theologians have covered by distinguishing between God's permissive will—the fact that God created a universe in which evil is possible—and God's decretive (or directive) will—those things which God actively does. The New Testament is clear that God is never the author of evil—so it is possible in the world he made, but it is not his intention for the world he has made.[26]

That is to say, human beings have a certain amount of independence that allows things to go wrong. Richard Dawkins thinks, and the late scientist Stephen Hawking thought, that we live in a deterministic universe. We do not.[27] God gave humans choice, and he remains sovereign—the Bible declares both clearly. Christians differ on exactly how that "works", and this is not the place to go into it. Our purpose here is simply to note that God is not taken aback by the coronavirus; he can work for good even in the evil of it, and his plans will not be thwarted by it, although in situations like the present crisis it can be very hard for us to take this on board. At the same time, we are responsible for our own responses to the crisis and to each other—for he has given us that freedom.

We live in a world where things go wrong, and where humans are able to choose to do wrong (or right). Why is the world this way? Here is the Bible's answer.

WHY THINGS ARE THE WAY THEY ARE

Think of it this way. When God created human beings to live in his "very good" creation, he endowed them with the marvellous gift of free will that made them into moral beings. Because of that, there was a possibility of moral breakdown through misuse of that freedom. And that is what happened—as the third chapter of the first book of the Bible, Genesis, so vividly depicts.

Genesis 3 says that human disobedience arose from a fundamental disagreement with God over the nature of life and the serious possibility of death. God had explicitly warned the first humans, Adam and Eve, that if they ate fruit from the tree of the knowledge of good and evil, which he had told them was off limits—in other words, if they acted in downright disobedience to him and independence of him—then they would certainly die (Genesis 2 v 17).

We need not discuss what the nature of the fruit of the tree was, or to wonder what quality it must have had so that eating it should produce the knowledge of good and evil. To interpret it that way is to miss the point of the story. To eat from any tree—indeed, to do anything at all, from whatever motive—that is contrary to the will and word of our Creator and the Ruler of this world is itself lawlessness. It is a frame of mind that asserts the creature's will against the Creator's—that pushes the Creator aside and makes central to everything the pursuit of one's own egotistical interests and interpretation of life. That is, in principle, what "sin" is.

And sin, as God warned those humans, automatically leads to death. There is nothing wrong with physical enjoyment or aesthetic pleasure in themselves—nor with the acquiring of moral wisdom and knowledge. But to suppose that these things are the sum total of life— to suppose that, as long as one can enjoy them, one can enjoy life to the full, independently of God and in neglect or defiance of his word—is a fundamental and tragic deception. God is not only the source of all the good things we enjoy; he is the supreme good that gives ultimate meaning and significance to all the lesser good gifts he gives us.

What happened in Genesis 3 was that the humans

rejected God, and sin entered the world. The consequences were huge. There was death—first in the spiritual sense of a rift in the relationship between humans and God, and, later, in the sense of physical death.

Moreover, nature itself was fractured by that same event—and that takes us back at once to our main theme. Genesis tells us that, upon their rebellion, though humans had to leave God's presence, they were not immediately ejected from their role of administrating the earth under God. They were allowed to keep their job of developing the earth's potential. At the same time, however, "creation was subjected [by God] to ineffectiveness, not through its own fault, but because of him who subjected it" (Romans 8 v 20).[28]

In the original Greek, the word for "ineffectiveness" (*mataiotēs*) carries the meaning that something is all "in vain": that is, it has not achieved the goal for which it was designed. When this passage says that creation was subjected to ineffectiveness and frustration "not through its own fault", it is referring to the curse God put on the ground because of Adam's sin:

"Cursed is the ground because of you [Adam]; through painful toil you will eat food from it all the days of your life. It will produce thorns and thistles for you." (Genesis 3 v 17-18)

That is, the fracturing of humanity's relationship with their Maker had consequences wider than for humans themselves. A rower in a boat who refuses to row in the correct way will affect not only themselves but also all the others in the boat—and may even damage the boat itself. Similarly, humanity's refusal to remain in the place assigned to them—made by God to know God and enjoy creation according to their Maker's laws—meant that God's very good creation became flawed and fractured.

There is, of course, no question that over the centuries there have been spectacular strides in the development of the earth and its resources. Yet success has never been complete: witness the many once-flourishing but now decayed civilisations of past centuries. Over and over again, nature has fractured and impeded human progress with thorns and thistles, backbreaking labour, pests, disease, epidemics, droughts, famines, earthquakes, volcanoes, and so on—coupled, sadly, with the destructive forces unleashed by selfishness, greed and moral corruption.

THE LINE DIVIDING GOOD AND EVIL

None of us can honestly discuss the problem of the world's evil and pain as though we were simply spectators of a phenomenon completely separate to ourselves.

The Russian author Alexander Solzhenitsyn, who was a survivor of Stalin's gulag camps, wrote:

> *"If only it were all so simple! If only there were evil people somewhere insidiously committing evil deeds, and it were necessary only to separate them from*

the rest of us and destroy them. But the line dividing
good and evil cuts through the heart of every human
being. And who is willing to destroy a piece of his
own heart? During the life of any heart this line
keeps changing place; sometimes it is squeezed one
way by exuberant evil and sometimes it shifts to
allow enough space for good to flourish. One and the
same human being is, at various ages, under various
circumstances, a totally different human being …
But his name doesn't change, and to that name we
ascribe the whole lot, good and evil." [29]

Solzhenitsyn was prepared to say openly what we all know intuitively: just as there is good and evil in creation, and in humanity in general, so there is good and evil in each one of us. We, too, are part of the problem.

The atheist philosopher John Gray gives unexpected support here:

"The cardinal need is to change the prevailing view
of human beings, which sees them as inherently
good creatures unaccountably burdened with a
history of violence and oppression. Here we reach
the nub of realism and its chief stumbling-point
for prevailing opinion: its assertion of the innate
defects of human beings.

"Nearly all pre-modern thinkers took it as given
that human nature is fixed and flawed, and in this
as in some other ways they were close to the truth

> *of the matter. No theory of politics can be credible*
> *that assumes that human impulses are naturally*
> *benign, peaceable or reasonable."* [30]

Here is an atheist essentially supporting the teaching of Genesis about the effects of the rebellion of human beings against God—about the reality of sin in the world.[31]

Once we grasp the fact that we are flawed, a more realistic formulation of the problem of moral evil might well be this: "I think and do evil. If, then, there is a God, why does he tolerate me?"

A DIFFERENT QUESTION

It is surely obvious that there are deep flaws both in human nature and in physical nature. The world is full of both violent and immoral human behaviour and earthquakes, tsunamis, cancers and the coronavirus pandemic.

Now, we can debate for ever what a good, loving and all-powerful God should, could or might have done. But experience shows that none of us has ever been satisfied with the outcome of that particular discussion.

The reason for this is that—no matter what we say—we are where we are and this is how the world is. We are all faced with the kind of mixed picture presented by a ruined cathedral—with all the beauty of the opening of a flower to the sun, and all the ugliness of a coronavirus destroying the human respiratory system.

As a mathematician, I am used to the fact that when we have tried, sometimes for many years, to solve a question without success, we begin to think that we might be better off looking at a different question.

And there is another question we can ask. If we accept—as we must—that we are in a universe that presents us with a picture of both biological beauty and deadly pathogens, is there any evidence that there is a God whom we can trust with the implications, and with our lives and futures?

5. Evidence of Love

We need convincing evidence of the goodness of God's character if we are to trust him. I would therefore ask you at this point to listen to the core of Christian teaching—whether you are familiar with it or whether it is new to you—and to try to understand it before concluding that belief in God is inconsistent with the existence of the coronavirus, or any other pandemic, disease or fracture in the natural world.

Christianity claims that the man Jesus Christ is God incarnate—the Creator become human. At the heart of the Christian message is the death of Jesus Christ on a cross just outside Jerusalem. The question at once arises: if he is God incarnate, what was he doing on a cross? Well, it at the very least means that God has not remained distant from human pain and suffering but has himself experienced it.

Therefore, a Christian is not so much a person who has solved the problem of pain, suffering and the coronavirus, but one who has come to love and trust a God who has himself suffered.

That, though, is only half of the story. If that suffering had been the end of what Jesus did, we would never have heard about it. But it was not the end. The message that set Jerusalem buzzing at that first Easter—the message that riveted the first-century world—was that Jesus had conquered death: that he had risen from the dead and would be the final Judge of humanity.

The importance of this cannot be overestimated. It addresses a fundamental difficulty that the atheistic worldview cannot cope with: the problem of ultimate justice. As we are all aware, untold millions of human beings throughout history have suffered grievous injustice and, after lives of misery, have died without any redress. No doubt that will also be true of some of the many victims of the coronavirus.

These people did not receive justice in this life. According to atheism, since death is the end, there is no next life in which justice could be done. If there is no final Judge, there can be no ultimate justice.

But the resurrection declares that justice is not an illusion and that our desire for justice is not futile. The abusers, terrorists and evil men and women of this world will one day be brought to justice. When I have tried to make this point to atheists, they often say that the thing to do is to work for justice in this world. I, of course, agree— working for justice is a Christian duty. But I also point out to them that this does not go any distance towards solving the matter of ultimate justice. Atheism, by definition, knows none. Atheism is an affront to our moral sense.

By contrast, the biblical view is that ultimate justice is very real. God is the authority behind the moral law, and he will be its Vindicator. There will, in consequence, be a final judgment, when perfect justice will be done in respect of every injustice that has ever been committed from earth's beginning to its end. Justice is not a mockery.

When the Christian apostle Paul lectured to the philosophers at the Areopagus Council in Athens, he told his audience that Jesus had been raised from the dead and appointed Judge of the world: a fact that guarantees that there will eventually be an ultimate answer to the deepest human questions.[32]

There is a human tendency to long for justice to be done, but there is also a tendency to react negatively to the message of ultimate justice, because it raises the question of our own position before God. "I couldn't believe in a God like that," some say, even as they protest at moral evil and accuse God of failing to intervene! Here is the problem with our natural response to God's future judgment: we welcome God's intervention only so long as it is an intervention in the lives of others and not in ours.

The fact is that we tend to see the evil in others, not in ourselves. So, when we think of what God should do, most of us would hold the view that God should be getting rid of the very evil people around us, but never us. After all, we are not as bad as all that.

The Bible teaches, though, that "all have sinned and fall short of the glory of God".[33] We have none of us kept our own moral standards, let alone God's—the Ten Commandments tell us that all too clearly.[34] Therefore, we all need a solution to the problem of the sin and guilt that—whether we know it or not—comes between us and God.

According to Christianity, that solution lies once more in the cross and the resurrection of Jesus. These events do not simply give us a way into the problem of evil and pain, and a resolution of the problem of justice. They show us what the name "Jesus" means—"he will save his people from their sins" (Matthew 1 v 21). Because of the death and resurrection of Jesus, those who repent of (which means "turn away from") their own evil and their own contribution to human pain and suffering— those who trust Jesus as their Lord—receive forgiveness; peace with the personal God who created and upholds the universe; a new life with new powers; and the promise of a world where suffering will be no more. Here Christianity does not compete with any other philosophy or religion—for the simple reason that no one else offers us forgiveness and peace with God that can be known in this life and endures eternally.

A Christian, then, is not a person who has solved the problem of suffering but one who has come to love and trust the God who has suffered *for them*.

TWO CROWNS

So how can this help us cope with disasters and pandemics?

The coronavirus is so called because it visibly resembles a crown ("corona" in Latin). A crown is a symbol of power and authority—and certainly this virus has colossal power over us humans. It is invisible to the naked eye, and yet just think about what it has forced many millions—indeed, billions—of us to do and not do.

It also forcibly reminds us of our vulnerability. It is easy to forget that we humans are mortal. The coronavirus is evidence that both our relationship with creation and creation's relationship with us are disordered; and that this is not an accident.

But hope is found in another corona: the crown of thorns that was forced on Jesus' head at his trial before his execution.

That corona shows us just how deep the break between creature and Creator goes. Earth is God's creation, not ours. We are not its owner, but we seek to be. We are only tenants and stewards, and flawed ones at that—many of us have made a mess of our own lives and even of those of others, to say nothing about what we have done to the planet. There cannot be two paradises for humans: one in fellowship with God and one without him. The coronavirus is very rapidly demolishing the illusion that we can build perfection on earth—and turning our initially lackadaisical, even complacent response into real fear, frustration and anger.

In a fractured world, damaged through the conse-quences of human sin, pain and suffering are inevitable. Perhaps we had hidden from this reality until coronavi-rus rampaged across the globe. Now we cannot ignore it, nor the big questions about life and death which it prompts. Here is C.S. Lewis again:

> *"We can ignore even pleasure. But pain insists*
> *upon being attended to. God whispers to us in our*
> *pleasures, speaks in our conscience, but shouts*
> *in our pains: it is His megaphone to rouse a deaf*
> *world."* [35]

Perhaps the coronavirus might function as a huge loudspeaker, reminding us of the ultimate statistic: that one out of every one of us dies. If this induces us to look to the God we may have ignored for years, but who wore a crown of thorns in order to bring us back into relationship with himself and into a new, unfrac-tured world beyond death, then the coronavirus, in spite of the havoc it has wreaked, will have served a very healthy purpose.

6. The Difference
God Makes

How should Christians respond to the pandemic? There are several different levels on which to answer this question.

HEED ADVICE

First, on the practical level, we would be wise to take heed of the best medical advice of the day. The problem that arises here is when that advice is not consistent, or when it is confused, as has been characteristic of some news broadcasting.

In order to reduce the spread of the virus, quarantine has been introduced for those people most at risk, especially the elderly and those with underlying medical conditions of the heart and respiratory system. Interestingly, in ancient biblical times, the Israelites were also instructed about the need for quarantine to prevent the spread of infectious illnesses. The Old Testament book of Leviticus even prescribed seven days isolation for some diseases, and an indefinite period for others.[36]

Responses of this kind, based on medical advice, are, of course, not an evidence of unbelief. God can protect us and heal us, but he expects us to be wise and use all the resources he has given us, including medicine. And social distancing is not an expression of selfishness but of loving one's neighbours enough to protect them.

Loving one's neighbour also means that those who are at little risk will have an important role to play in visiting (where circumstances and regulations permit) the vulnerable, helping them with their shopping and providing much-needed company, even if their time is limited.

MAINTAIN PERSPECTIVE

C.S. Lewis once wrote a fascinating article about how Christians should respond to the existence of atomic weapons. I reproduce it below; but, to help us apply it to our own situation, I have inserted "coronavirus", "virus" or "pandemic" in square brackets at the relevant points to give the idea (slightly imperfectly, I admit, and I apologise for that):

> *"In one way we think a great deal too much of the atomic bomb [coronavirus]. 'How are we to live in an atomic [pandemic] age?' I am tempted to reply: 'Why, as you would have lived in the sixteenth century when the plague visited London almost every year, or as you would have lived in a Viking age when raiders from Scandinavia might land and cut your throat any night; or indeed, as you are already*

living in an age of cancer, an age of syphilis, an age of paralysis, an age of air raids, an age of railway accidents, an age of motor accidents.'

"*In other words, do not let us begin by exaggerating the novelty of our situation. Believe me, dear sir or madam, you and all whom you love were already sentenced to death before the atomic bomb [coronavirus] was invented: and quite a high percentage of us were going to die in unpleasant ways. We had, indeed, one very great advantage over our ancestors—anaesthetics; but we have that still. It is perfectly ridiculous to go about whimpering and drawing long faces because the scientists [coronaviruses] have added one more chance of painful and premature death to a world which already bristled with such chances and in which death itself was not a chance at all, but a certainty.*

"*This is the first point to be made: and the first action to be taken is to pull ourselves together. If we are all going to be destroyed by an atomic bomb [coronavirus], let that bomb [virus] when it comes find us doing sensible and human things—praying, working, teaching, reading, listening to music, bathing the children, playing tennis, chatting to our friends over a pint and a game of darts— not huddled together like frightened sheep and*

thinking about bombs [viruses]. They may break
our bodies (a microbe can do that) but they need
not dominate our minds." [37]

This is tough reading, but it reminds us that Christian faith gives us a different perspective.

LOVE YOUR NEIGHBOUR

Third, we are called to love. At the beginning I listed some of the earliest pandemics of which we have knowledge. What I did not say at that point is that we also know something about how the Christian community responded to them. In a recent article entitled "Christianity Has Been Handling Epidemics for 2000 Years", Lyman Stone, a research fellow at the Institute for Family Studies and an advisor at the consulting firm Demographic Intelligence, wrote this:

"Historians have suggested that the terrible
Antonine Plague of the 2nd century, which might
have killed off a quarter of the Roman Empire, led
to the spread of Christianity, as Christians cared
for the sick and offered a spiritual model whereby
plagues were not the work of angry and capricious
deities but the product of a broken Creation in
revolt against a loving God.

"But the more famous epidemic is the Plague of
Cyprian, named for a bishop who gave a colourful
account of this disease in his sermons. Probably

a disease related to Ebola, the Plague of Cyprian
helped set off the Crisis of the Third Century in
the Roman world. But it did something else, too:
It triggered the explosive growth of Christian-
ity ... Cyprian's sermons told Christians not to
grieve for plague victims (who live in heaven),
but to redouble efforts to care for the living. His
fellow bishop Dionysius described how Christians,
'Heedless of danger ... took charge of the sick,
attending to their every need.'" [38]

Nor was it just believers who noted this reaction of Christians to the plague. A century later, the actively pagan emperor Julian would complain bitterly of how "the Galileans" would care for even non-Christian sick people, while the church historian Pontianus recounts how Christians ensured that "good was done to all men, not merely to the household of faith".[39] The sociologist and religious demographer Rodney Stark claims that death rates in cities with Christian communities may have been just half that of other cities.[40]

This habit of sacrificial care has reappeared throughout history. In 1527, when the bubonic plague hit the German city of Wittenberg, Martin Luther (the founder of the Reformation) refused calls to flee and protect himself. Rather, he stayed and ministered to the sick. The refusal to flee cost his daughter Elizabeth her life. But it also resulted in a pamphlet, "Whether Christians Should Flee the Plague", in which Luther

provides a clear articulation of the Christian response
to the epidemic:

> *"We die at our posts. Christian doctors cannot*
> *abandon their hospitals, Christian governors*
> *cannot flee their districts, Christian pastors*
> *cannot abandon their congregations. The plague*
> *does not dissolve our duties: It turns them to*
> *crosses, on which we must be prepared to die."*

Stone's article concludes with the following statement:

> *"The Christian motive for hygiene and sanitation*
> *does not arise in self-preservation but in an ethic*
> *of service to our neighbour. We wish to care for*
> *the afflicted, which first and foremost means not*
> *infecting the healthy. Early Christians created*
> *the first hospitals in Europe as hygienic places*
> *to provide care during times of plague, on the*
> *understanding that negligence that spread disease*
> *further was, in fact, murder."*

None of this is to say that we should ignore the rules
being put in place to slow down the infection spread
and so put ourselves (and others) at unnecessary risk,
especially in situations where we have to self-isolate
or where we are in an area that is locked down. It is to
say that we should be looking for how we might love
others, even at cost to ourselves—for that is how God
has loved every Christian in the person of his Son, by

dying for them on the cross. Loving our neighbour also means avoiding that selfish, hysterical attitude to food and basic necessities that leads to empty stores and our neighbours having to do without.

REMEMBER ETERNITY

This gives us a window into an aspect of the Christian legacy that is often forgotten. For, fourth, Christians need to remember about eternity. The early Christians, living as they did in a dangerous world where they were surrounded by all kinds of threats and where life expectancy was relatively short, were given strength to live as sacrificially as they did, contributing so much to the wellbeing of others, by the fact that they had a real and living hope that went beyond the grave.

C.S. Lewis once wrote about this in words that are as apposite today as when he wrote them:

> "A book on suffering which says nothing about heaven is leaving out almost the whole of one side of the account.

> "Scripture and tradition habitually put the joys of heaven into the scale against the suffering of earth, and no solution of the problem of pain which does not do so can be called a Christian one. We are very shy nowadays of even mentioning heaven. We are afraid of the jeer about 'pie in the sky' … but either there is 'pie in the sky' or there is not.

If there is not, then Christianity is false, for this doctrine is woven into its whole fabric. If there is, then this truth, like any other, must be faced..." [41]

The pioneer Christian apostle Paul was not ashamed to mention his convictions and confidence regarding the future:

"I consider that our present sufferings are not worth comparing with the glory that will be revealed in us ... For I am convinced that neither death nor life, neither angels nor demons, neither the present nor the future, nor any powers, neither height nor depth, nor anything else in all creation, will be able to separate us from the love of God that is in Christ Jesus our Lord." (Romans 8 v 18, 38-39)

These are not the words of an armchair philosopher at ease in his study, but of a man who had seen and experienced life at its roughest and toughest. Paul unjustly suffered frequent beatings and imprisonment, on occasion being left for dead, and along the way experienced much deprivation and hardship.

At times, like Paul, I try to imagine what that glorious heavenly realm is like. Here is the question which arises within me: if the veil that now separates the seen and the unseen world were to be parted for a moment and we could see the present state of those who have died— the myriads of innocent Christian believers who suffered from the horrendous evil perpetrated by immoral governments, war lords and drug barons, or who have been innocent victims of natural disasters and pandemics—is it just possible, in the light of all we know about Jesus Christ, that all our concerns about God's handling of the situation would instantly dissolve? We have not yet reached that other world, but we do have a message about it that comes from it—a message that this virus-infected, anxious world desperately needs to hear.

THE CLIMB

But who am I to write about such things? I am painfully aware that some, perhaps many, who will read these words may well have lost a loved one recently. You may feel "What does he know about it?" All I can say to this is that there are people who know far more than I do about real pain and suffering, and who can therefore show more understanding for your loss, and assure you that there can be hope despite it. I want to close by quoting from a remarkable book called *I Choose Everything*, in which Jozanne Moss (in South Africa) and Michael Wenham (in the UK) describe their journey through pain. They are both suffering from a terminal illness (motor neurone disease), and have only met by email.

Jozanne likens that journey to climbing a mountain. With honesty and courage, she writes about how God has sustained her:[42]

> *"I have been climbing my mountain for about fifteen years. Most of those years were spent in the base*

camp at the foot of my mountain where I knew God was preparing me. I was always afraid to climb and thought that the base camp was my goal. I didn't think I could make it to the top, but God showed me through my illness that it wasn't about me, or what I could do. It was always about him. 'It is God who arms me with strength and makes my way perfect. He makes my feet like the feet of a deer; he enables me to stand on the heights.' [43]

"I finally left the base camp and started my ascent. God has chosen Everest for me. It definitely has not been easy, and my foot has often slipped. I have often felt weary and at times I didn't think I could go any further. Parts of this climb are very steep and far beyond anything I could achieve, but he continues to show me his power and strength, and when I'm tired, he is there. '… but those who hope in the Lord will renew their strength. They will soar on wings like eagles; they will run and not grow weary, they will walk and not faint.' [44]

"My climb is nearly over. I think I am near the summit of my mountain. The higher climbers go, the closer they get to the summit, the harder it becomes to breathe. The oxygen level decreases as the altitude increases, which causes climbers to suffer from altitude sickness. (According to the Internet: 'Symptoms of mild and moderate *altitude sickness typically consist of headache, shortness of breath, sleeping trouble, loss of appetite, nausea and rapid pulse.') As the muscles of the body weaken with the progression of Motor Neurone Disease so too do the muscles necessary for breathing become weaker. I feel short of breath, have regular headaches, have trouble sleeping and often experience a very rapid pulse. But it doesn't worry me because I know I am nearly at the top of my mountain. The climb is becoming tough now, but I must press on. The reward that awaits me when I complete the climb, far outweighs any sacrifice one makes. Ask any mountain climber!*

"So here I stand, looking up. The end is in sight and my heart races with excitement. I look forward to the day when I can say: 'I have fought the good fight, I have finished the race, I have kept the faith.'" [45]

Those last words are the words of the apostle Paul, who added:

"Now there is in store for me the crown of righteousness, which the Lord, the righteous Judge, will award to me on that day—and not only to me, but also to all who have longed for his appearing."

(2 Timothy 4 v 8)

One day, Jesus will appear. It will be the day that he promised his disciples long ago when he said to them:

"Peace I leave with you; my peace I give you. I do not give to you as the world gives. Do not let your hearts be troubled and do not be afraid. You heard me say, 'I am going away and I am coming back to you.' If you loved me, you would be glad that I am going to the Father, for the Father is greater than I." (John 14 v 27-28)

"I am coming back to you," he said. And John, who recorded these words, tells us later of what Jesus will bring with him on that day: nothing less than a new creation.

"Then I saw 'a new heaven and a new earth,' for the first heaven and the first earth had passed away, and there was no longer any sea ... and God himself will be with [his people] and be their God. 'He will wipe every tear from their eyes. There will be no more death' or mourning or crying or pain, for the old order of things has passed away."
(Revelation 21 v 1, 3b-4)

The coronavirus and all the plagues that have ravaged the world will be no more: the crown of righteousness that will be given to those who love the Lord Jesus will never perish or fade.

Peace in a pandemic? Only Jesus can give that. The issue for all of us is this: will we trust him to do so?

Postscript

D o I think I have answered all the questions that this crisis has raised? No, I don't. Far from it. I am personally left with many ragged edges and issues on which I would like to have more clarity. One day I shall have it:

"For now we see only a reflection as in a mirror;
then we shall see face to face. Now I know in part;
then I shall know fully, even as I am fully known."
(1 Corinthians 13 v 12)

In the meantime, I shall follow the advice of the great nineteenth-century preacher Charles Haddon Spurgeon:

"God is too good to be unkind and He is too wise to
be mistaken. And when we cannot trace His hand,
we must trust His heart." [46]

I hope that reading this has persuaded you to do that; or, at least, that it has shown you that the God who wore a crown of thorns is worth some more of your time and thought. I hope that you will investigate more fully whether he might indeed be the one who can give hope and peace, whatever the months and years to come may bring.

ENDNOTES

1. *Report of the WHO-China Joint Mission on Coronavirus Disease 2019 (COVID-19)* (Feb. 2020).
2. "NIH Director: 'We're on an Exponential Curve'" in *The Atlantic,* 17 Mar. 2020.
3. mphonline.org/worst-pandemics-in-history (accessed on 20 Mar. 2020).
4. citizen.co.za/news/south-africa/courts/2256298/pray-in-groups-of-no-more-than-70-twice-a-week-for-the-sake-of-sa-mogoeng (accessed 20 Mar. 2020).
5. "God vs. Coronavirus" in *The New York Times,* 10 Mar. 2020.
6. theguardian.com/world/2020/mar/13/first-covid-19-case-happened-in-november-china-government-records-show-report (accessed 23 Mar. 2020).
7. *Crime and Punishment* (Clayton, 2005), p 233.
8. *Collected Letters, Vol. 3,* (New York, 2000), p 520. Lewis is not saying here that creatures—humans—literally become God. He is rather referring to the fact that becoming a Christian through trusting Christ means that we are brought into God's family as his sons and daughters (see John 1 v 12-13; John 3 v 1-21).
9. *The Universe Next Door* (IVP, 2010).
10. Karma (in Hinduism and Buddhism) is the sum of a person's actions in one of their successive states of existence, which is regarded as deciding their fate in the next.
11. Job 42 v 7-9.
12. Job 1 v 13-19.
13. See, for example, John 9 v 1-3.
14. 1 Corinthians 11 v 20.
15. *Dialogues Concerning Natural Religion,* part 10 (1779).
16. *River Out of Eden* (Basic Books, 1992), p 133.
17. *The Brothers Karamazov* (1880), book 11, chapter 4.
18. "Time to Stand Up" (Freedom From Religion Foundation, 2001).
19. *Virtue Ethics* (New York, 1991), p 2-3.
20. *The Will to Power* (1888), p 389.
21. *Twilight of the Idols* (Penguin, 1990), p 80-81.
22. *The Gay Science* (Vintage, 1974), p 282.
23. *The Miracle of Theism* (Clarendon Press, 1982), p 115-116.
24. weforum.org/agenda/2015/11/are-viruses-actually-vital-for-our-existence (accessed 20 Mar. 2020).
25. *Rare Earth* (Springer, 2000).
26. James 1 v 13.
27. I have dealt with this matter in considerable detail in my book *Determined to Believe?* (Lion Hudson, 2017).
28. Translation by D W Gooding MRIA.
29. *The Gulag Archipelago* (Collins, 1974), p 168.
30. *Black Mass* (Farrar, Straus, and Giroux, 2007), p 198.
31. See my *Gunning for God* (Lion Hudson, 2011), chapter 7, for more detail on this issue.
32. Acts 17 v 31.
33. Romans 3 v 23.
34. Exodus 20 v 3-17.
35. *The Problem of Pain* (Geoffrey Bles, 1940), p 81.
36. Leviticus 13 v 1-46.
37. "On Living in an Atomic Age" in *Present Concerns: Journalistic Essays* (1948).
38. foreignpolicy.com/2020/03/13/christianity-epidemics-2000-years-should-i-still-go-to-church-coronavirus (accessed 20 Mar. 2020).
39. As above.
40. As above.
41. *The Great Divorce* (Signature Classics, 2012), p 427.
42. *I Choose Everything* (Lion Hudson, 2010), p 176-178.
43. 2 Samuel 22 v 33-34.
44. Isaiah 40 v 33.
45. 2 Timothy 4 v 7.
46. goodreads.com/quotes/1403154-god-is-too-good-to-be-unkind-and-he-is (accessed on 20 Mar. 2020).

thegoodbook
COMPANY

Thanks for reading this book. We hope you enjoyed it, and found it helpful.

Most people want to find answers to the big questions of life: Who are we? Why are we here? How should we live? But for many valid reasons we are often unable to find the time or the right space to think positively and carefully about them.

Perhaps you have questions that you need an answer for. Perhaps you have met Christians who have seemed unsympathetic or incomprehensible. Or maybe you are someone who has grown up believing, but need help to make things a little clearer.

At The Good Book Company, we're passionate about producing materials that help people of all ages and stages understand the heart of the Christian message, which is found in the pages of the Bible.

Whoever you are, and wherever you are at when it comes to these big questions, we hope we can help. As a publisher we want to help you look at the good book that is the Bible because we're convinced that as we meet the person who stands at its heart—Jesus Christ—we find the clearest answers to our biggest questions.

Visit our website to discover the range of books, videos and other resources we produce, or visit our partner site www.christianityexplored.org for a clear explanation of who Jesus is and why he came.

Thanks again for reading,

Your friends at The Good Book Company

thegoodbook.com | thegoodbook.co.uk
thegoodbook.com.au | thegoodbook.co.nz | thegoodbook.co.in

WWW.CHRISTIANITYEXPLORED.ORG
Our partner site is a great place to explore the Christian faith, with powerful testimonies and answers to difficult questions.